Instructions for using AR

LET AUGMENTED REALITY CHANGE HOW YOU READ A BOOK

With your smartphone, iPad or tablet you can use the **Hasmark AR** app to invoke the augmented reality experience to literally read outside the book.

1. Download the **Hasmark app** from the **Apple App Store** or **Google Play**

2. Open and select the (vue) option

3. Point your lens at the full image with the and enjoy the augmented reality experience.

Go ahead and try it right now with the Hasmark Publishing International logo.

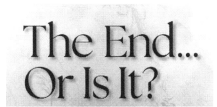

The End...
Or Is It?

ENDORSEMENTS

This book is a MUST read if you've lost someone you love. Sandy guides you to understand death, heaven and the spirit realm in such a down to earth way. She is absolutely the real deal!

~ **Maureen Hancock**,
World renowned medium,
Best-selling author of *The Medium Next Door*

What a powerful and emotionally moving book! Sandy dives into the delicate (and often scary) topic of death and the Spirit realm and brings you a whole different perspective...one without fear. Bravo! The world needs this!

~ **Irene Weinberg**,
Host of Grief and Rebirth Podcast;
Author of *They Serve Bagels in Heaven*

The End...Or Is It reminded me how close God and my loved ones in Spirit are. Sandy's words helped me remember things I knew in my heart, but grief wanted me to forget. If someone you love has passed, READ THIS BOOK!

~ **Kenny Morrell**,
Musician, Songwriter,
Recording Artist

The End . . . Or Is It?

A Medium's guide to unf*ck your mind about death.

SANDY ALEMIAN

Editor: Jamie Geidel jamie.geidel@gmail.com
Cover Design: Anne Karklins anne@hasmarkpublishing.com
Interior Layout: Amit Dey amit@hasmarkpublishing.com

ISBN 13: 978-1-77482-187-9
ISBN 10: 1774821877

DEDICATION

This book is dedicated to you, the reader.

I don't know what has brought you to this book or what loss you've gone through in your life.

I don't know what you were taught when you were a kid or how long you've had questions inside you about death or Spirit.

But I see you.

I see you when you put on a smile for the world, but inside is a different story.

I see when you try to make believe that you're okay when you're really not.

I see when you feel crazy because your beliefs don't mirror the people around you or when you roll your eyes when people try to push their religious beliefs about heaven and hell.

I see you because I was you.

I'm so glad you're here.

This book is for you.

TABLE OF CONTENTS

INTRODUCTION

When we lose someone we love, there are so many questions.

Are they okay? Where are they? Why did this happen? How do I live without them?

And without the right answers, we make up a story in our head. These stories keep us in pain.

Not everything you may have been taught about death or heaven is true. In fact, a lot of what you might have been taught may have f*cked up your mind about death, heaven, and Spirit.

A recent client of mine told me she got scared if she ever noticed a floral scent around her. She thought it must be from an evil spirit because she had been taught that when you smell flowers, it means that someone's going to die.

See what I mean?

I don't want you to live with untruths. They stem from fear and cause too much pain.

I want this book to help you see death differently because when we no longer fear death, we no longer fear life.

I also want you to know that you can not only have one more conversation with your loved one who has passed, but you can also have a continued relationship with them the way they are in Spirit.

My intention is to share what I've learned from the almost thirty years of having conversations with Spirit as a medium.

I will share beautiful and amazing client stories that will explain life and death from a different perspective.

And on a side note . . . when you see the word *God* in this book, please feel free to substitute Source, Creator, Pure Love, or whatever word works for you.

With so much love,
Sandy

CHAPTER 1

WHY IS DEATH SO SCARY?

If I knew then what I know now about the world of Spirit,
I wouldn't have tried so hard to save so many people.

~ a heart surgeon in Spirit

If you google images of death, 99% of what you'll see are black and grey pictures of skulls, crossbones, skeletons, graves, grim reapers, angels of death, tears, and knives. No wonder death doesn't feel welcome or warm and fuzzy.

Death feels like the enemy. It can feel like a personal attack when we lose someone we love. It feels like it happens *to* us. They *left* me. God *took* them from me. From our human perspective, death isn't supposed to happen unless someone is very old or very, very sick. And we typically feel sorry for the person who died because they'll miss out now.

Death is a taboo subject. It makes a lot of people feel uncomfortable.

I'm curious about you. Feel free to write your answers here.

What were you taught about death from religion when you were a kid? Write your thoughts here.

How was death dealt with when you were young?

Was there an early experience you had with loss that shaped your beliefs?

Draw a picture of what death looks like to you.

This is the image of death you've been carrying with you. It might not even be yours . . . it might have been given to you.

How does this image feel to you?

What effect does this have on how you live . . . or how you approach love, relationships, your heart?

We didn't talk about death when I was a kid. It was something that grown-ups discussed. What I understood was that it was the end. It was sad. It was not a good thing. It made people upset. When someone died it was like a big black hole swallowed them up. They disappeared and went to heaven *up there* with God.

Heaven never felt reachable for sure. It was so far away.

I was so scared of death that I used to cry myself to sleep so many nights as a kid, afraid of something happening to one of my parents. I remember praying, "God, please let me be in my 20s when something happens to them." Then when I reached my 20s, it changed to "God, let me be in my 30s when something happens to them," thinking I'd be better able to handle it.

My dad died when I was 45, and my mom recently passed. I *did* handle it better. Not because of my age. It was because of what I had awakened to after losing my infant daughter, Talia, when I was 33 years old.

Talia was born perfectly healthy, or so we thought. On day two, she started having seizures. The next 2 1/2 weeks were overtaken with testing and waiting, waiting and testing. Every test was normal except for her EEG, which showed no normal brain activity. Her brain wasn't able to give directions to the rest of her body, telling it what to do. So, they concluded that she'd never be able to see, hear, laugh, smile, walk, talk . . . nothing. She was on a ventilator because even her breathing was compromised. She stayed in the hospital for the duration of her life.

It was the most harrowing roller coaster ride of my life. I turned to my writing to help me process what I was going through.

I began receiving messages through my journal writing. Messages that told me that I was going through this for a reason and that I would be helping many people through this experience. Honestly, I had no idea how I was going to get through each day.

Talia died at 31 days old. It was her short little life and death that broke me open to having conversations with God. I learned how to tune into the realm of Spirit. It was the absolute worst time of my life, and yet it was the biggest spiritual growth spurt of my life.

In the year after she passed, I needed to understand all about death and Spirit. I went on a journey to learn how to tune into Spirit and became a spirit medium. Now, I have a different perspective of death . . . and life. I still grieve when someone I care about dies. I just know how to tune into their energy, and it helps the grief to shift.

FROM MY JOURNAL

God, why are we so afraid of death?

> Many experience death as the ultimate separation. They feel separate from their loved ones. And while this is true on a physical level, their loved ones in Spirit are still as connected with them spiritually as they were when they were here. The only thing that is missing is the body. And that is where many who have experienced loss become stuck. They assume: I can't see them, I can't hear them, I can't feel them. They must not be here with me.
>
> Though this can be your experience, please know that there is a different experience possible for you. It is one where you have an awareness that death does not take your loved one away from you. It takes their body away from you. But what is left? Their beautiful Spirit essence that cannot be killed, cannot be harmed, and does not die.

CHAPTER 2

ARE WE JUST A BODY?

Right before I died, I was in and out of my body. I was so free.
I was happy that I was about to be done with it!

- a client's daughter in Spirit who passed from cancer

The global fashion market was worth $1.5 trillion in 2021.[1]

The global cosmetics industry was worth $534 billion during 2022.[2]

The global gym industry was worth $96.7 billion in 2020.[3]

Shocking, isn't it? Especially when you remember that the body is temporary.

[1] Milica Arsenovic, "31 Absolutely Stunning Fashion Industry Statistics and Facts," May 26, 2022, *Capital Counselor*, https://capitalcounselor.com/fashion-industry-statistics

[2] "Beauty & Personal Care – Worldwide," *Statista*, last accessed September 22, 2022, https://www.statista.com/outlook/cmo/beauty-personal-care/worldwide

[3] Smiljanic Stasha, "19+ Statistics and Facts About the Fitness Industry (2022)," May 20, 2022, *Policy Advice*, https://policyadvice.net/insurance/insights/fitness-industry-statistics

We identify this body. We put so much time and energy into taking care of our body, feeding it, clothing it, grooming it. It's only a teensy fraction of what we really are.

What are we? We are a spiritual being having an experience in a body. So, we *are* spirit energy, and we *have* a body. Until we don't.

Before we were born, we existed as energy, and after we leave this body, we exist as energy.

So, we are always energy, and sometimes we have a body attached to it.

This energy can never be harmed, doesn't get hurt, and does not die. It is our spirit.

The reason we don't often feel it is because we're tuned into our physical being in this physical world more than we are tuned into our inner spirit.

When you meditate, you can feel the peace and the inner calm of your spirit. It's your beingness, your presence, your essence. It's there, whether you feel it or not.

> My client brought her 14-year-old daughter to my office, so she could connect with her grandmother in Spirit. This grandmother shared,
>
> "Make sure you understand the difference between who I was when I was there with a body and what I'm like now."
>
> She nudged me to look at the granddaughter's cute pink and black plaid shoes. She said to her granddaughter,
>
> "When you wiggle around your foot like that, it looks like the shoe is moving. When you take the shoe off, the shoe doesn't move. You realize that it wasn't the shoe that was moving by itself. The foot was making the shoe move. That's like me and

my spirit energy. My energy made my body move. But I'm not my body, just like your foot is not the shoe. When you take your shoe off, your foot doesn't stop existing. When I took my body off, I didn't stop existing."

My client asked, "Sandy, what should I do with the ashes? I really want my mom to be happy where she ends up."

So, I asked her mom in Spirit.

"I'm already happy where I am. Remember, the ashes are the remnants of my body. It's not me. Do what feels right for you in your heart. I'm right here, and I'm ok."

My daughter's friend's dad was in a non-responsive state before he died. She asked me if I could connect with him to see what he wanted to say.

"My body is like my car. I am not my car. I got in my car to get me around. When I got out of my car, I didn't go away. I stepped out of my car. When I leave my body, I'm not going away . . . I'm stepping out of my body."

I told her I thought it was an odd (but cute) analogy with the car.

Then she said, "Sandy, he loved his car more than anything!"

CHAPTER 3

WHAT IS DEATH?

Tell my husband that cancer didn't take me.
It just took my body.

Each year, 60 million people die. Death. We all do it eventually.

The hard part for us when we lose someone is that we are so used to identifying with the physical. I know that if I see you, you're right here with me. If I can hear your voice, you're here. If I can touch you, you're in the room with me. When someone dies and becomes nonphysical, we are at a loss. We can't see them, touch them, feel them, or physically hear them. But . . . that doesn't mean they're not with us.

We look for signs everywhere. We wait for a visitation in a dream. We look for them in our physical world. All the while, they are energetic beings who are still connected to our hearts.

They're not attached to their body anymore. They're free.

While we go into grief because we are missing the physical aspect of them, they are in a pure positive state of being.

They see death so differently.

So, what *is* this thing called death?

Death is not the end of the journey. It is the end of the journey with the body. When someone we love dies, it's as if they unzip from the body and become aware of their pure spirit again. It is only the body that dies.

Spirit has given me an acronym for the word death.

D-Divine

E-Expansion

A-And

T-Total

H-Healing

They've expanded back into pure positive divine energy. And in that frequency, there is no fear, no worry, no pain, no dis-ease, no suffering.

They are pure love. (Yes, even if they weren't that on earth.)

> A woman came to my office to connect with her elderly mom in Spirit. When I made the connection, her mom said, "Tell my daughter I love being dead!"
>
> I mentally told this mom that I couldn't say that to her daughter. She insisted.
>
> "Tell her I love being dead!"
>
> So, begrudgingly, I shared what I was hearing. She screamed!
>
> "Oh, my God, that sounds just like what my mom would say!"

This mom was sharing how much she loved being out of her body because she'd been so sick when she was here. Luckily the daughter understood where her mom was coming from.

The day after my dad died, I was at my mom's house, and connected with his spirit for my mom and my four sisters. He asked me to bring his spirit through for the whole family before his memorial service.

A few days later, our entire family got together at my mom's. I was a little nervous, all eyes on me, waiting to hear what Papa had to say. He reassured us all that he was ok and offered beautiful reassurances.

I loved the message he had for all his grandchildren.

"When you see me in the casket, remember that that's not me . . . it's just my body!"

My dad also gave an interesting message directly to my mom.

"Roxy, pay attention to one ring on the phone."

We didn't really know what that meant. A few weeks later, she called me.

"Sandy honey, I don't know what to make of this. I was sitting here with Nancy, and the house phone rang. I went to answer it, but it only rang once. So, I picked up the phone and pressed caller ID."

The caller ID read *Alemian, Zarven* (that's my dad's name!), and then it had our home phone number.

"Wait a minute. The home phone called the home phone, and it only rang once??"

"Yes, honey, do you think that was Daddy?"

"YES!" I screamed into the phone.

I don't know how he did it, nor do I need to understand how he did it. I was so happy that my mom got that sign from my dad, letting her know he was with her.

A couple of months after he died, I got another one of these phone calls from my mom.

"Sandy, I think I'm going crazy."

I hear that a lot from my clients, and I don't think anyone is crazy when they tell me their spirit stories. There are experiences that we can't explain or understand. It doesn't mean we are crazy.

My mom was 80 at the time, but a very vibrant 80-year-old. So, I asked her why she thought she was going crazy. Here is the backstory:

My mom's routine every morning was to get up early, make a cup of coffee, and sit at the computer. She'd play computer games that usually involved winning a "jackpot" of points (not money)! When my dad was here and she would win a jackpot, my dad would get so excited for her and say, "Atta girl, Rox!" My mom and dad had a very close relationship. They were married for 56 years and deeply loved each other.

So, on this *am-I-crazy* morning, she was having her coffee, playing Hog Heaven on the computer, and she won a jackpot.

"Sandy, I turned to the picture of Daddy that's right here on the kitchen table and told him, 'Zav, I just won a jackpot!' As soon as I did that, the kitchen lamp blinked three times. So, I walked over to the lamp, and asked it, 'Zav, is that you honey?' Sandy, the lamp blinked three more times. Am I going crazy or what?!"

My heart smiled.

"No, Mom. I think that was Daddy letting you know he's with you and that he loves you."

My mom is now with my dad in Spirit. She died after she turned 94. She is always with me, and I know I can have a conversation with her spirit. *And . . . I miss her physical presence.*

Sometimes when I'm driving around town doing errands, I feel the urge to pop in and see her. Other times I'll reach for my phone to call her and then remember she's not physically here. Those moments feel icky. I feel the sadness of her not being here physically. Then I remember that she's with me always, just in a different form.

If you're interested, I did a three-part video called, *Hi Dolly!* that's on my website www.sandyalemian.com. It describes how, as a medium, I went through the before, during, and after of her death. Have a tissue handy. :)

CHAPTER 4

CAN I GET SOME ANSWERS?

Imagine being underwater where it's cloudy and dense. You can't really see where you're going. Being in spirit is like coming up for breath above the water. You feel so free!

~ A client's mom who struggled with lung cancer
before she died

When someone we love dies, and we have unanswered questions, they linger in our minds and won't leave us alone. I have found that the unanswered questions we have after someone dies are what cause us pain. It's what keeps us up at night. It's the not knowing that keeps us stuck. The questions make us squirm.

If you ask others what they think, you'll get different answers based on their belief systems.

If you ask a priest or a minister, you'll get an answer that is in alignment with that religion.

I'm offering you answers that are in alignment with Spirit.

Here we go . . .

When someone dies, are they okay?

Remember, there are two parts to who we are. There's the physical part of our body, and then there's our spiritual energy. We're always spirit energy. Sometimes, we have a body that goes along with that.

When someone dies, their energy leaves the physical body. They become aware of pure love. Any dysfunction of the body or the mind doesn't go with them. No more disease, addiction, Alzheimer's, dementia, depression, or the like.

They're not suffering. They're not sick. They are so much more than okay.

> Two sisters came to see me. Their brother had just died by suicide three weeks prior.
>
> He had left notes for his family, telling them how much he had loved them. He left his house carrying a gun he owned. He drove to work and packed up his stuff there. He drove around all day. His family couldn't reach him, so they called the police.
>
> At about six o'clock that night, the police saw his car and pulled him over as he was driving back into his hometown. He pulled the trigger on himself as the policeman approached the car.
>
> When I connected with his energy, he showed me that as soon as he shot himself, he found himself with his family. He was trying to reach out to them to let them know he was okay, but he couldn't because of all the hysteria.
>
> He wanted me to share with his sisters what he had felt during his last day. He explained his emotional pain and how he had

thought that he had been a failure for a good part of his life. He then asked if I would be with him in the energetic place where he now was.

When I agreed to go there with him, he brought me to a place that felt dark. It wasn't scary. It was just dark. He appeared to have black armor on, like a knight's armor. I sensed that armor was the protective barrier he had put around himself while he was here.

He said he wasn't scared. He also shared with me that he knew his mom was somewhere near him in Spirit, but he hadn't yet seen her.

As I was witnessing him in this darkness, I wanted to help him. "Can you hold the thought of God right here, right in this darkness?"

"That's not going to work for me. I didn't believe in God."

His sisters confirmed . . . he was an atheist. I tried a different angle. "Can you hold the thought of love right here, right in this darkness?"

"That's not going to work for me either. I didn't love myself. I don't know what love is. I don't know what self-love is."

And then a thought occurred to me.

"Hold the thought of the love that you have for your wife and your two kids."

As soon as I said that to him, there was a light that was now coming through the grated mouth area of the armor. I could see this light that was now starting to stream from within. I knew something was happening and encouraged him to keep going.

"You are doing great. Keep this up. Keep holding the love that you have for your wife and your two kids."

As he did that, it was almost like there was a shot that went POW! from within the armor. Now there was light pouring out from inside the armor.

"Keep doing it. You are doing great!"

Inside my mind, I heard sounds of POW, POW, POW . . . Little explosions were happening, and so much light was now pouring out from the armor.

Suddenly, his dark armor was breaking apart into little bits and pieces, and before you knew it, the entire armor had disintegrated. All that remained was an amazing light.

"I did it! I did it! I did it! I remembered who I am. I remembered that I AM the light. I couldn't do this on earth because I couldn't break through this armor."

The armor represented the idea of failure, the lack of self-worth that he had felt when he was here.

His sisters told me that a lot of people had been praying for him since he had died. They were afraid that he was in purgatory or hell. I asked him why all those prayers didn't help him remember this light.

"All of those prayers were coming to me from people's place of fear. They were afraid of where I was, and they were praying out of fear. You helped me to remember from love and from light, and that's how I remembered who I am.

And my mom is right here. She was waiting for me this whole time, but she was waiting for me in the light. I couldn't see her, but now I do.

Please tell my family not to take responsibility for my death. Each person feels responsible for different reasons. My daughter is thinking, 'If only I were enough.' My wife is thinking, 'If my love were enough . . .' My sister is thinking, 'If only I could have seen the signs' because she was a substance abuse counselor. And the policeman is thinking 'It is my fault. If I hadn't stopped him, maybe he would still be here.'"

Nothing could have stopped his death. He did the very best that he could with the tools that he had. He was fighting with his mind and couldn't fight anymore. He's no longer battling his inner voices. He is out of the fight and in the light.

And at some point, he will go through a life review. He'll be able to experience what his death felt like from everybody else's perspective. He'll have an opportunity to see his life and his death very differently. At some point, he may choose to come back into another lifetime to see how he could go through some of the same issues, but go through it differently, with more self-love and compassion.

I wonder how many of us are fighting against our own minds. How many of us put on emotional armor to keep us from being hurt by life? We don't need to die to release our armor. We need to remember love and light. Love heals all.

What was interesting is that the night before I had connected with this gentleman for his two sisters, I had worked with another client whose mom had also died by suicide five years prior. As I was connecting with her energy, she said that after she passed, she felt like she was in a place of darkness.

"It wasn't scary. It was dark. I don't remember how long I was there because there is no time in spirit. As soon as I thought of God, a light appeared. I realized the light was coming from me and the more I thought about God, the more that light enfolded me. Then I realized it was my own light that I went into. My light isn't separate from God."

If only we could remember that more while we are living. It would make life easier for us. When we think we are separate from God, we struggle. No matter how much we forget, we can always remember once again.

Are they together?

Yes. Heart connections are heart connections. Love doesn't die. And are you ready for this? Even people who didn't get along here have said that there's no more bickering, no resentment, no hatred. Only love.

How do you find them when you die?

This is a wonky concept to describe, but Spirit says, "You just do." Soul energies will draw themselves together, like two magnets, because of their soul history together. They've also described that you'll find each other through vibration, like tuning forks that begin to vibrate together.

What about people I don't ever want to see again? Will they be there too?

You may have run into a person or two or twelve and have been grateful that your relationship (workwise or personal) is over! Done! This is coming from pain and hurt . . . and you don't take that pain into Spirit with you.

In Spirit you'll see the light of all those who were on your path. You may not have seen their light in your human interactions (especially if they hurt you). In Spirit, there's no anger or resentment. There's only love.

Do they feel bad if we don't visit them at the cemetery?

A woman came to my office with her daughter. Her husband had been in Spirit for about three months. The first thing he asked me to say to his wife was "Honey, please don't feel guilty for not visiting me at the cemetery."

As a medium, that's a fairly generic thing for me to hear, but I had to share it anyway. She started sobbing! It surprised me.

Then she explained.

"Sandy, since my husband had passed, I visited him at the cemetery every single day. But for the last couple of weeks, I haven't gone, and I have felt so guilty."

What he said to her in response was one of the most adorable things I'd heard from Spirit.

"Honey, if you go to the cemetery, I go to the cemetery. If you don't go to the cemetery, I don't go to the cemetery."

Does it matter to them whether we cremate or bury the body?

Spirit has said that once they release their spirit from the body, they don't care what we do with the body.

My client's mom was in Spirit.

"Sandy, I feel so bad. When my mom was here, she told us she wanted to be buried. We ended up having her body cremated instead. I'm so afraid that she's angry that we had her cremated."

I connected with her mom's spirit energy. She said, "It doesn't matter to me what you did with the body because that is not who I am!"

If someone was in a coma, did they know that we were with them?

Those in Spirit have said that often they can go in and out of the body while waiting for the body to shut down. They've said that they are aware of who was in the room, the kind of energy that was in the room, whether it was loud or soft, and so forth.

> My client was walking down the street with her sister and her young son. A car careened towards them and hit the fence that they were walking by. The fence fell on top of them. When help arrived, her son somehow ended up in her arms. They both survived, though she was temporarily in a coma. Her sister was killed.
>
> She came to see me get some closure on what had happened. She wanted to connect with her sister. I asked her if she was willing to allow me to guide her into a connection with God and Spirit. She agreed.
>
> I brought her into a relaxation first and guided her back to the accident. She went back to what it was like being in a coma.
>
> "I couldn't feel my legs after the accident."
>
> "What happened after that?"
>
> "I go to the ocean. I'm in the presence of God. It's warm, comforting--no pain."
>
> "Notice how you can move about."
>
> "Everything is very light."
>
> "Ask God who was there. Who saved your son and put him in your arms?"
>
> "I think it was my dad. Male . . . family member."
>
> "Ask God about your sister's death."
>
> "It's about patience, and tolerance . . . compassion."
>
> "Was this your fault?"

"No."

"Could you have stopped this?"

"No."

"Did you fail to protect anyone?"

"It was not in my hands. I feel bad that I couldn't take some of the pain from my sister."

"Ask God if it could have been different."

"God says, 'No.'"

"The part of you that still feels guilty, what does it look like?"

"It's big. It protects me. If I hurt myself with some pain, at least I'd be in some pain like my sister."

"Ask God, are you meant to hold onto this guilt as some loyalty to your sister?"

"No . . . it's not serving anyone by holding onto it. This guilt . . . it's dark, ugly, distorted, looks angry. It's been there for years."

I wanted to ask this guilt a question and asked my client to allow guilt to have a voice.

"Guilt, why do you stay?"

"I like the power. I control her. I own her."

"Are you willing to leave?"

"Not without a fight."

I guided my client to bring God's energy in. "Allow God to be in the presence of this guilt. What happens?"

"Guilt weakens in the face of God."

"Let it face God."

"It's not scary anymore. It tells me it's hiding from God."

"Why?"

"Fear of letting go."

There was a long pause.

"Sandy, God is healing it. I see blue eyes. It feels like it's my sister in Spirit. This feels wonderful. There's no judgment, only peace. It's like lace blowing in a breeze. This is where I was for a week when I was in my coma. There's no pain."

I began addressing her as she was reliving her experience in the coma.

"Is there anyone else there with you?"

"Yes, but no faces. It's everyone who had loved me and already passed. They were part of who I was. They tell me they love me and that all will be well. I don't want to leave them. It's unconditional. I'm weightless. I'm not in my body."

"Are you attached to anything going on with your body?"

"No, I'm not in it. I'm not attached to what's happening with my body. I'm at peace."

"Can you sense the prayers that were being said for you?"

"I don't really like it . . . feels like worry to me. I would have to own that, and I don't want to. I want them to stop worrying and go about their business so I can just be. I can sense if someone is afraid or worried. I don't have to fix it."

"Do you try to tell anyone on earth anything?"

"I tell them that I'm ok. I do that through light . . . a blue light."

"Does Spirit tell you why you went through this?"

"To grow."

"Was the accident planned?"

"Yes, for my growth."

"What about the people in the car? Were they chosen for this as well?"

"Don't know. I have anger at God. I didn't understand the hurt towards my sister and my son in order for me to grow through it."

"Were your sister and son part of the plan?"

"Oh wow. Yes, they were."

"Was it also for their growth too?"

"Yes."

"Is there anything to be angry at?"

"No, not at all."

"When you know this, what happens to your anger?"

"It fizzles. When you understand that everything is for your growth, there's no need to be angry at anything. Then you have to allow for growth."

"Is there anything that could help facilitate the growth further?"

"Willingness to grow. Insecurities are blocking my growth."

"What understanding would help you to let go of them? What is the truth that would release all insecurities?"

"Unconditional love . . . no judgment."

"Do you feel that from God?"

"Yes. Completely. It's huge."

"Be immersed in it. Notice what it does to your insecurities."

"What insecurities??"

Maybe part of our human dilemma is that we don't connect with God's unconditional love more.

"When you are fully immersed, are you any different from God?"

"No. I am that light."

"And when you can remember that you are the light, what happens to worry and fear?"

"There is no worry, no fear. Things are as they should be. I'm surrounded by that light. All different colors. Purple is awesome; yellow is warm. Green is rich. There's no brown. So many colors I've never seen. It's like the most beautiful butterfly."

What is the process of dying like for them?

Death brings the separation between the physical body and the spirit. The body can go through all kinds of things. The body experiences the accident. The body experiences illness or disease. The body experiences trauma, but the spirit doesn't feel anything. The spirit can't be damaged or harmed and does not feel pain.

We see their suffering; they don't hold on to that. They disconnect from the body, and they start becoming much more aware of their pure positive spirit energy. That's why they don't feel the pain.

If it's been a sudden impact, like a car accident, as soon as the accident happens, they are out of the body.

Mom, I flew out of my body, so quickly,
I didn't even feel the impact.

~ A client's young son in Spirit

In one of my private sessions, I was working with a family whose son had passed. He was crushed by a machine at work and his family was tormented by the image of what it must have been like for him when he died.

He said, "I don't remember going through any pain. I remember that my body went through something, but I'm not holding on to what that was like for me. Please remember me as I am now. Connect with me as I am now, not what you imagine must have happened to my body. That will keep you in pain."

Is it ever too soon to try to connect with Spirit?

Some mediums say that you should wait three to six months. I have found that it's not so much that Spirit needs the time to adjust. It's those who are grieving who might need some time to process the loss before they connect.

Sometimes when clients are deep in grief, they won't be able to absorb what Spirit is giving them. The pain feels too big. One client came to see me two weeks after her husband died in a motorcycle accident. She sobbed through the entire session. He was telling her he was okay and gave me details to make sure she knew it was him. She couldn't really process what I was saying because her pain was still so raw.

It's normal to cry during a session. It's a tender time for your heart and your emotions. You'll know when you're ready to make a connection. Trust that.

Can anyone connect with Spirit?

I believe so. But the mind will get in the way. It takes a desire, some quiet time, and a willingness to open up and trust. I'll show you later in this book how you can have a conversation with Spirit through your writing.

What does Spirit do all day?

I love this question. This is a concept that's really, really tough for us to understand from our human perspective because we are so ruled by time. There's no time in the vibration of Spirit. There are no days, hours, minutes, weeks, months, or years.

We are human beings, but most of us are human *doings*. In Spirit, we are spiritual *beings*. In Spirit, we create with thought and experience it in no time. The same is true while we still have this body. We create with our thoughts, and often we talk ourselves right out of the very thing we'd love because of doubt or fear.

> *In my heaven, I can have the feeling like I'm still hunting deer, but after I catch anything, they come back to life right away!*
>
> ~A client's brother in Spirit

Do they miss us?

Spirit has shown me that they imagine our spirit with them in their heaven. They bring us to their heaven! So, from a spiritual perspective, nothing's missing. We, on the other hand, are still in the physical, so we miss their physical presence.

Their physicality is and was only a small part of who they were, and it's only a small part of who we are. When we tune into our inner spirit, that's where we can feel, hear, or sense their spirit. In that moment, their spirit fills that void.

A mom in Spirit wanted to explain to my client (her daughter) what she experienced when she died.

"There was a light beyond anything I've ever experienced. I knew it was God. It was absolutely overwhelming. There was no fear. There was no worry. I didn't always know God was available for me when I was alive in my body.

I'm not missing anything. I'm not missing my rings. I'm not missing my body. I'm not even missing my kids because I bring their spirit into my heaven in every moment. I just wish they knew that and could feel it too. They wouldn't miss me so much."

When someone dies, what do they first experience?

When we die, whatever we thought heaven would be like is what we'll *first* experience. If we believe that we'll experience Jesus and the angels, or a bright light, that is what we'll experience.

If we believe that we are going to hell, then an idea of hell might be the very first experience. In a split second, however, we are given an opportunity to see it differently. If someone didn't believe in God, in Spirit, they've said that they have an experience with "light" which feels like the most beautiful love they've ever encountered.

My client's mom died by suicide. She jumped from the top of a building in Boston.

"When I first passed, it felt like I was in a place of turmoil. I didn't know how long I'd been there, but then I was shown a light. It was the energy of love. I had a choice. I could stay in my own turmoil, or I could go to the light. I somehow knew that if I chose the light, the turmoil would be gone. It's what I chose. Please tell my daughter this because she's still in turmoil since my death. She can choose again too. I want her to shift."

When you die, you blend back into God. There is never, ever any separation between who you are and what God is. Death is about being reborn back into truth.

~ A Spirit dad's message for his children

Can they feel our thoughts?

I recently worked with a client whose brother had struggled with addiction and then passed. He told a lot of lies throughout his life. As a result, he had a tough life here. Apparently, he hadn't treated others particularly well either. When I connected with his spirit, he shared with me that he could feel the energy of what people were saying about him. Some were saying some nice things about him, and some were saying unkind things about him.

"It's like I am holding a blank white canvas. People's words are like paint splats. The nice comments have much lighter colors and the negative comments have darker colors. I'm not attached to positive or negative thoughts. I can see the colors of them.

I can actually see that a person's thoughts are more about the person thinking them. If there is forgiveness inside someone, that comes through their thoughts. If there's resentment, that's what comes through. I can see myself differently now. Their thoughts don't affect me."

If Spirit is always around us, do we have any privacy here?

Yes. Spirit is nonphysical energy, so they don't have physical eyes to see us. What that means is they're not seeing you naked in the shower and they're not seeing you in your more intimate moments.

So how do they watch over us?

They feel our energy. It's like our emotions are different colors. They can "see" our colors and "feel" our emotions but it's more of a telepathic knowing. They've said that when our energy feels low, they send us love. If we get quiet and our hearts are open to receive, we may feel a sense of peace wash over us.

What should we do with their stuff?

Trying to figure out what to do with their stuff can feel rather emotional. Sometimes it feels like if we let go of their stuff, we'll be letting go of them. That is simply not true . . . it's a lie we tell ourselves.

Spirit is no longer attached to their clothing or shoes, their house, their ashes etc. Do whatever feels right in your heart. Not once in all the years of working with Spirit have they *ever* expressed any disappointment in anyone for giving away or throwing away anything that belonged to them. They are pure positive energy, and they're always connected to our hearts.

Do they hear us?

Yes. It doesn't matter whether we talk to them out loud or in our heads. Language starts out as thoughts. And when we talk to them, we are sending thoughts to them. They receive the vibration of our thoughts telepathically and send thoughts back to us the same way.

Is it okay if we're angry at them?

Getting angry at a loved one who has died might be exactly what we need to do as part of our healing process. If we suppress it, it can lead to depression. Because the spiritual realm is a vibration of love and light, anger doesn't hurt them. Stored anger and resentment hurt us.

What do they need from us?

I was guiding a client to make a connection with his mom in Spirit. I brought him into a relaxed state of mind. "What would you love to ask her?"

"She always loved chocolates, so this past Valentine's Day, I left her a box of chocolates at her gravesite. I want to know if she knew that."

"So, ask her."

"Mom, did you get the chocolates I left you on Valentine's Day?"

Immediately, he began laughing. "What did she say?"

"She said, 'Yes, but how the hell am I supposed to eat them?'"

Spirit doesn't need anything from us. They don't need a shrine. They don't need us to go to the cemetery. They don't need us to hold a religious service for them. They don't need us to get a tattoo for them.

We do those things for *ourselves*. It makes us feel better. Sometimes it makes us feel close to them.

Spirit has said we don't have to do anything to honor them. And they have said they don't need our prayers. They are already in a place of pure love.

They've said that *we* are the ones who need our own prayers!

Prayers have energy. They make us feel better, like we're doing something to help our loved one. When we pray for someone who has passed, they redirect the energy of that prayer back to whomever needs it. So, your prayer to someone in Spirit may be affecting someone else who really needs it. How cool is that?

> *The best prayer you can ever offer to anyone*
> *(living in a body or not) is a heartfelt "I love you."*

Can Spirit help us win the lottery?

I was conducting a small group event, *Messages from Heaven*, a few years ago. One of the women in the group jokingly asked if Spirit could give her lottery numbers.

"That is not how Spirit uses me!" I replied.

Immediately after I said that, six numbers rolled out of my mouth, along with the date August 16th.

"That's never happened before, so do whatever you want to with them."

I doubted that they meant anything.

My sister was there that night and wrote the numbers down. She called me, my mom, and a couple of my sisters the next day to give us the numbers. My work with Spirit is about bringing through a healing perspective, not getting lottery numbers, so I wasn't going to do anything with them.

A teensy part of me wondered . . . *but what if?* So, I played every combination of those numbers in all the lottery games in Massachusetts on that date. I was thinking about what a cool story it would be if I won.

Well, none of the number combinations won. None. I wondered why Spirit did that. I felt stupid.

A couple months later, my sister who had been at the group event said to me, "Sandy, do you remember those numbers you gave out at that group that night?"

"Yes, and none of them came out!"

"Well, the woman who asked you for the numbers took them to Foxwoods casino on August 16th and won $1000 in Roulette!"

Yup. I kid you not. And another story about the lottery . . .

> I was booked to do a private group for a woman whose son died the year prior. I'd met with her family twice at my office, and her son's spirit had come through beautifully. The woman asked if I'd come to her home to do a session for about twelve of her son's friends. They were struggling to process his death. As I was drying my hair, (and running a little late) I sensed he was right there with me.
>
> "Stop and get my mom some candy on your way."
>
> "Ooh, I can't. I'm sorry. I'm running late!"
>
> "Stop and get my mom some candy."
>
> "Ugh, ok, I will."
>
> On the way to her home, I stopped at a convenience store and randomly picked out some candy for her. The woman in front of me at the register was picking out some scratch tickets.
>
> "I'll take a number 3 ticket, no, a number 5 ticket, give me two number 8's . . ."
>
> She was taking so long, and I was feeling anxious about keeping the group waiting.
>
> Finally, it was my turn to pay for the candy I'd picked out. I was a little aggravated and wanted to be rewarded for my extra effort. Ugh.
>
> I thought I'd make a deal with this boy in Spirit.
>
> "Ok, I'm doing this for you. Can you tell me which scratch tickets to get?"

I quietly heard the numbers 8 and 33, so I bought the scratch tickets labeled with those numbers.

I arrived at the mom's home, apologized for being late, and shared that her son wanted me to stop and get candy for her. She started crying.

"Oh my God, Sandy, I have this one special candy dish that I always had filled up with candy for Chris and his friends. It's been empty since he died. I guess he wants it filled for his friends."

She took the bag, opened it, and shrieked. "You even got Peppermint Patties! They were his favorite!"

My heart felt glad to be able to do this for this boy in Spirit. The night was awesome. For each of his friends, he came through with details of funny experiences that they had shared. It was one of my best experiences as a medium.

When I got home, I was so excited to scratch the lottery tickets to see what I had won! I knew for sure that I'd be rewarded somehow!

Nothing. Absolutely nothing.

I laughed. It reminded me that working with Spirit isn't about the money. I receive something that money can't offer—joy in bringing through Spirit's energy and perspective, and witnessing the healing that people receive from it.

Are children able to sense Spirit?

Absolutely. Kids are often sensitive to spirit energy, especially before they start feeling like it's not "normal." When a young child talks about having an imaginary friend, it might not be imaginary at all. If a parent doesn't understand the energy of Spirit or has fear around it, they may bring that fear to the child. The child might then shut down their innate intuitive ability.

Is there any such thing as an accidental death?

When someone dies, it is their time to transition, according to their soul contract. Even if it is an accidental death.

Spirit has said that we have a few different potential exit points on our soul contract. And that when we are close to an exit point, our soul determines whether to stay or whether to go. That won't make sense to our human mind, especially when it's a young person that dies.

What about murder? That couldn't have been planned, could it?

According to Spirit, even a murder was first held as a potential in somebody's soul contract.

Sometimes a murder has a huge impact on a family or a community, which can bring a shift into forgiveness or compassion. Remember, Spirit doesn't see their own death as a bad thing. They see it as *I'm free. I'm out of my body now.* They see it as part of the game of life.

This won't make sense from the level of our human understanding. It will make sense when we can get the soul's perspective of not just this lifetime but past ones as well. All the dots connect.

Can we communicate with pets in Spirit?

I've had sessions where animals have come through from Spirit for my clients. If someone had to put a pet to sleep, the pet said they were grateful that they could die with dignity. Pets can communicate telepathically just like your loved ones in Spirit can, through thought energy.

After a client's mom passed, her cat started acting very odd.

"Sandy, I swear my mom is now my cat."

How adorable is that? While our loved one's energy in Spirit can influence your pet's behavior, they don't "jump into" your pet's energy so they can interact with you. They communicate with you telepathically. It's up to us to listen.

What about suicides?

Those who have died by suicide have come through beautifully in a Spirit session.

They've shown me that it's like they put a bubble around them right before they made their decision. In that bubble, all they can feel is pain, confusion, or turmoil. In that bubble, they aren't able to rationally think about the family that they would leave behind. All they think about is, "I just want to be out of this pain."

The best thought they could reach for? "The only way out of pain is to get out of this body."

In all the years of connecting with Spirit, not once has anyone who has died by suicide ever come through and said that it was anybody's fault or that someone should have (or could have) stopped them.

At some point after they leave their body, they're given an opportunity to experience a life review. They've shared that they can see the thoughts that kept them in pain. And they can see that those thoughts were all lies they believed.

They see how they could have done it differently. They seem to make mental notes about how they will handle obstacles and challenges differently next time around.

They're not punished for ending their life. In Spirit, they are healed. They want us to heal too.

> I remember a young man in Spirit who came through for his family in my office. He wanted me to experience what it was like for him to be out of his pain, and he gave me an analogy, which I thought was adorable.

"At Thanksgiving when you've eaten so much, you're uncomfortable in the pants that you're wearing. You cannot wait to unzip your pants when you get home! When you finally get to do so, it brings such relief. That's what it was like for me when I released myself from my body and from my mind. I was able to find peace that I couldn't find in my life."

When someone has a physical or emotional challenge, do they still carry that with them into Spirit?

No. Spirit is free from any limitations. They remember that they went through limitations, but they don't feel the effects from them anymore.

Before we come into this life, our soul chooses a physical body that will suit us best to experience the growth and lessons we've agreed to. If it's a severe disability, the growth is for everyone else around them. Growth can look like unconditional love, patience, compassion, and acceptance.

While we're here physically, there's so much that can affect the body and the mind (illness, disease, pain, emotional distress, hurtful memories), but nothing affects your spirit. Your spirit is that part of you that is one with God. It's the part of you that can't be damaged, cannot be harmed, and does not die.

I want to mention Alzheimer's. What Spirit has said to me is that Alzheimer's is so much harder on the caregivers than it is for the individual who has it. It's hard watching a loved one slowly forget who we are.

They'll typically convey how happy they are to be out of that body because the mind stopped working for them. They describe how wonderful it is to be free and whole again.

They've also shared with me that Alzheimer's was actually a gift. It gave them an opportunity to stop replaying painful memories or past dramas over and over again in their mind. It gave them a semblance of mental or emotional peace before they died. And sometimes Alzheimer's helped them revert back to being like a child and receive the love they may not have received as a child earlier in their life.

Are they jealous or upset if I go into another relationship or get married again?

> "We know how much you love us and that no one could take our place. We don't feel jealousy in this vibration. We hold only love. You're imagining what our human personality would feel. Our souls are always connected, and we know how much you loved us and how much you still love us."

> A client's husband was in Spirit. He asked me to tell his wife that it was okay with him if she wanted to date again.

> "Oh, that can't be from my husband. He would never say that if he were here."

> She was absolutely right. If he were here physically, of course he'd be jealous and wouldn't want her to be with another man. But he's not here physically, and she is. She still has physical needs and desires, and he wanted her to know that he was absolutely wanting her to feel fulfilled.

There's no judgment on when you can start dating, or when it's ok to have a new companion or partner. Whether you wait a week, a month, a year, or five years, Spirit is not hurt, upset, or jealous. Your loved one wants you to be happy.

> Two siblings came to see me to connect with their mom in Spirit. The younger sibling (who had just graduated from high school) was really upset that his dad had started dating. He knew for sure that his mom was hurt and upset about it. Here's what she said to him.

"When you graduate from high school and you enter college, your college experience doesn't erase any of your high school experiences. It's just the next chapter of your life. This is how I want you to see Dad dating. It doesn't take away anything from me or his love for me. It's the next chapter of his life. I will always be your mom; I'm always here for you and will guide you if you let me."

Her son finally felt some peace, knowing that his mom was always going to be with him, even if his dad was in another relationship.

The stories we convince ourselves of do more harm to us than good. The truth sets us free.

Do we have to come back into physical form again after we die?

Some clients have said, "Sandy, there's no way I'm ever coming back to earth again. It's too hard. I never want to go through this again."

I totally understand that. When we go through a difficult time, it's hard to see that there's a gift or any growth that could come from the experience. It's hard to remember that we have a soul contract, where we've agreed (on a soul level) to go through any obstacles in life. We set it all up ahead of time to see how we can move through life with more love and compassion.

When we are in Spirit, we remember that God's energy lives in us and that there is no separation from God, or Spirit. We also remember that spiritual wisdom is embedded within us. But when we come into a body, we tend to forget all that.

Spirit has said that this life is like a game of hide and seek. We hide the energy of God within, then seek that love and peace in other people, jobs, things, and money (the world "out there"). We experience pain, drama, and darkness. We are broken open; we can get bitter or better. Within any life challenge is an equally powerful awakening to remember that love and peace is within us and no one and nothing can take it from us.

When we awaken to this, life gets better and better.

CHAPTER 5

A LITTLE TIME OUT FOR YOU

How we see death will determine how we live our life.

In Chapter 1, you did some writing about what the mind has been con-ditioned to think about death. Let's check in again.

Place a hand on your heart and take a few deep breaths. Take your time with this.

What do you know deep down inside to be true about death? What resonates with you?

Write your thoughts here.

What does that feel like in your body?

Look at how it may feel differently compared to your original writing about death.

Both perspectives are within us at the same time. One may make us feel scared and anxious, one will hopefully help us to feel peace.

CHAPTER 6

HEAVEN . . .
WHAT AND WHERE?

Heaven is not a place we go to, but rather
a state of consciousness.

As children, most of us were taught:

Heaven is somewhere "up there" in the clouds with God. When you die, you'll go "up there" too.

Unless your religion taught about purgatory or hell.

I told a recent client that I was writing this book, and she wanted to share some things she was taught in parochial school about heaven and hell.

"Sandy, at 5 years old, we were taught that God could "get" you at any time. If you missed Mass on Sunday, you were going to hell.

If you wore shorts to church, then you were going to hell.

We were all 'bad.' If you weren't that bad, you were going to purgatory. But if you converted someone, you automatically would go to heaven. If you got divorced, you'd go to hell. If someone had a son and he became a priest, the mother would automatically go to heaven."

Wait, what??

See how our minds can get f*cked up?

In larger audiences when I ask participants to point to where heaven is, most people still raise their arm and point up.

From Spirit's perspective, heaven is not a place. It is a state of consciousness that holds no illness, no challenges, and no death. Heaven is the energy of pure love that is always accessible (unless you believe otherwise). They've said that "hell" is what we experience here on earth. Life feels like hell when we feel disconnected from love.

A client recently said to me, with tears in her eyes, "Sandy, I talk to my husband in heaven all the time. I didn't think it was possible to hear from him or anyone in heaven because they just seem so far away." It was a validation of why I needed to write this book.

> A client came to see me after her uncle died. "Sandy, I really want to know if my uncle gets the music that I play for him."
>
> I asked the uncle, and all I was sensing was a big "thumbs up." I didn't understand what the whole story was about.
>
> She said, "Whenever I go to the cemetery to visit my uncle, I always bring his favorite music, loaded up on my iPod. I kneel down at his grave, put the iPod headphones on the ground, and play his favorite music really loudly so that he can hear it inside his grave."

As she was speaking, I could feel her uncle standing beside me, laughing. Not laughing at her but laughing at how adorable the gesture was.

He asked me to say to her, "Honey, just know that when you're kneeling down and you have the headphones on the ground, I'm smiling and saying, 'What the hell are you doing . . . I'm not in there! I'm standing right beside you!'"

What were you taught about heaven from parents or religion?

Write your thoughts here.

Tune into your heart . . . what do you know to be true in your heart about heaven?

What images come to you?

What does that feel like?

CHAPTER 7

WHY CAN'T I SENSE MY LOVED ONE AROUND ME?

Please tell my dad that I am with him every night.
And when he wakes up in the morning, sometimes
he remembers it and calls it a dream.

W e live in a loud, busy, distracting world. Our thoughts and attention may be focused on other things. We are attached to our cell
phones, laptops, and social media that are constantly dinging and noti-
fying us of something that needs our attention. Whatever is getting our
attention is what we'll experience.

Spirit energy is often subtle; Spirit thoughts are quiet.

Our emotions can also be a barrier to not feeling Spirit. If we're feeling sad, worried, guilty, afraid, or upset, those emotions can cloud our
connection.

Our spirit is always connected with our loved ones' spirits. It's like a
beautiful web of light.

And you don't have to wait until you die to know this.

You don't have to be perfect; you don't have to go through any special rituals, meditate for days, or sit on a mountain top in order to feel, sense, hear, or communicate with Spirit. What it takes is an intention to get quiet and listen.

> My client's 23-year-old son died of an overdose. This dad felt like he had failed his son. When I tuned into the young boy's energy, he shared this with me.

> "I'm trying so hard to help my dad, but I can't get through to him because he's carrying around so much guilt. Please tell him to let go of the guilt. He didn't fail me! I'm really okay."

There is so much wisdom that we can receive from the non-physical realm. Tuning in to Spirit can help ease the pain that is in our hearts and help release burdens that we carry. You can free yourself from guilt, worry, anger, fear, and sadness. Once you ask Spirit a question and receive the truth, the truth sets you free.

Write your thoughts after each question.

What were you taught about connecting with Spirit?

Are there any fears that you have about connecting?

What questions do you have for your loved one in Spirit?

CHAPTER 8

ARE YOU WILLING TO LISTEN?

Though you may feel lonely, you are never ever alone.

My connection to the realm of angels started about thirty-five years ago. I have many journals of messages from my team of angels. Interestingly, I was never warned that I'd go through the loss of an infant. And I understand why. If they had warned me what was up ahead for me, I'd have lived in such fear every day. And I'd probably have chosen a different path and stopped at one child. Talia's death changed me. It opened me up to a realm of so much love. And I am forever grateful.

I started having real back-and-forth conversations with the energy that I call God when Talia was in the NICU at Beth Israel Hospital. It is what truly saved me and brought me peace in the most challenging time of my life. You can read about these experiences in my first two books, *Congratulations . . . It's an Angel* and *WHAT was God Thinking?!*

My first conversation with Talia was two and a half weeks after she died. It came through my writing. It had been the toughest day so far. I went for a walk because I wanted to clear my head. It didn't work. When I got home, one of my sisters called and encouraged me to sit and try to write. I really was at my lowest of low points.

Sitting on my bed, I held a yellow pad of paper and a pen, thinking to myself: "I have nothing inside of me." I couldn't possibly imagine any inspiration coming through me to help me to feel better. But as I sat there on the bed with my pen, a thought whispered inside my head that said, "Mommy! Mommy! Mommy!"

I couldn't write that. I thought I was going crazy. Then I heard it again. "Mommy!" Again, it wasn't an audible voice that I heard; it was more of an internal thought. I didn't want to fight it, so I just wrote "Mommy" on my paper.

This is what followed:

> "Mommy, please know that I'm okay. There is so much love here that I'm never alone. There's no suffering or heartache. You'll see me again, although I'm not far from you now. My love is always surrounding you. Can you feel that peacefulness during times of great despair? That's us, taking care of you. Time isn't relevant anymore, so don't think that it's going to be so long before we'll be together again. I felt all the love from everybody at the hospital. Even though I wasn't able to show it physically, I tried to give something back to each one of you. Remember the quiet times we had and cherish those times alone."

This message brought me such peace that I hadn't felt in a while. I had no doubt it was from Talia.

You might be wondering how she could communicate, since she was an infant. This message was from her spirit . . . not from her baby body. Spirit has no age.

My client's dad was in a coma before he passed. My client wanted to know if God was talking to his father while he was in the coma. His dad said, "God was talking to me from the moment I was born and never stopped . . . I just didn't know how to listen."

I want to teach you how to listen . . . and receive.

We're not always the best listeners. We're busy, we're distracted, and so many things are vying for our attention.

We can have a conversation with someone *face-to-face*, and *as* they're talking to us, we're not present. Maybe we're thinking about an argument we had earlier. Maybe we're looking at a speck of something in their teeth. Maybe we're in our head, trying to figure out what we want to say to them next. We've not heard a word they've said.

We spend most of our lives with a physical awareness. When you look in the mirror, you see your hair, and your face, and your body, and your clothing. It's how you typically see others and relate to them as well.

When we put our attention and our focus on our work or the news on television, that's what our attention will be on, and that's where our experience will be.

When someone comes into the room, we know they're there because we can see them with our physical eyes, we can hear their voice with our physical ears, and we can reach out and touch them.

This is how we relate to others in this world—with our physical senses. And with our focus and attention.

Imagine trying to communicate with Spirit, who is not in physical form. It may feel like we're talking to the ceiling.

Now imagine Spirit trying to communicate with us when *we're* not present.

We've got to meet them halfway.

It's possible. It's doable.

So, take a moment and contemplate . . .

> You are an energy of light here.
>
> That that light doesn't ever go out.
>
> It is within you, whether you can feel it, sense it, or not . . . it is there. It's always there.
>
> Somewhere inside of you is light.
>
> This light is connected to the light of God, to the light of your loved ones in Spirit.
>
> You're always connected . . . even now.
>
> Take a deep breath.
>
> Read this slowly: **I am a spirit energy having a physical experience.**

CHAPTER 9

WHAT ARE YOU AFRAID WILL HAPPEN?

I'm not back there in the memories…
I'm right here with you.

- a client's son in Spirit

I've shared that we are all connected with Spirit, and conversations with them are entirely possible. Here are some common beliefs (none are true) that my clients have had that can block having a real conversation with Spirit.

1. *They're just gone. Dead is dead.*

A while ago, a dear friend of mine whose wife had passed said to me, "Sandy, for the 6 months after she died, I kept asking for signs from her. We had a great marriage, and I know she'd want to try to contact me, but I got nothing. So, I decided that there is nothing that exists after death."

That felt so sad to me. He wasn't open to learning to try another way of connecting with her. He didn't want me connecting with her. His heart was closed.

2. *It's not possible. Maybe other people can do it, but I can't. I've tried.*

Stop your noise. You can.

3. *I'm afraid of what they might say. What if they're upset or disappointed in me?*

Remember . . . Spirit doesn't do anger or judgment anymore. To have someone disappointed in you means they'd have to have expectations. They don't have expectations. They don't do disappointment. They are in the energy of pure love, and that is where they share from.

If you're afraid that Spirit is either upset or disappointed in you, you're projecting what you're feeling onto them.

4. *I'm angry at them.*

The emotions we hold on to can bring us into a lower vibrational state. Spirit energy is a high vibration of energy. So, it's not that you are further apart from Spirit when you're holding onto those emotions, but those emotions may interfere with your receptivity to connecting.

If you're angry with them, it might be why you would want to get their perspective now. Getting a different perspective will help you find truth, which truly does set us free. The stories we hold onto from old fights and resentments can all be cleared up, if you let them.

Sometimes people imagine the person who has passed to be exactly the same way that they were here on earth. They're not. They'll project their personality to me as a medium, so you'll know it's them, but in truth, they are the energy of love.

5. *I don't want to bother them.*

You're not. Get over it. :)

6. *Connecting with Spirit is the devil's work.*

Oh Lordy, can we please get past this one? Certain religions teach that it's wrong to connect with Spirit. I remember back in the early days, when I was first letting it be known that I was a spirit medium, every once in a while, I would get an email from someone who would write: "Do you know that this is the devil's work that you're doing?" And they would quote some Bible scripture.

Then I'd pray, "God, if you don't want me doing this work, please block it. But if you want me doing this work because of how it brings healing to people, please bless it."

It has been blessed for almost 30 years now.

7. *What if I get nothing? I'll feel worse.*

Don't give up. Keep showing up for Spirit. Release the fear and do it anyway.

So, my friend, is there any resistance that might get in your way of having a conversation with Spirit?

Journal your thoughts here . . .

Place a hand on your heart and ask, "What do I know deep down inside to be true about this?"

CHAPTER 10

HELLO . . . IS THIS THING ON?

You're always connected to us in Spirit,
but you're not always tuned in and open to receive.

W hen we lose someone we love, we miss talking with them, getting their advice, and even working through unfinished business. We wonder, "Are they proud of me? Are they really ok?"

I hear all the time from my clients. "Sandy, I wish I could have one more conversation."

Some people are aching to have a dream of their loved one that might give them a message.

Those dreams are great, but they seem to happen so randomly. And most of us may not remember our dreams in the morning.

I don't want you to have just one more conversation. I want you to have real back-and-forth conversations with them. Not just of *you* talking to *them*. But the kind where you're able to ask questions and receive answers.

So how do you do that?

Remember, Spirit is non-physical energy; those who have passed use non-physical communication . . . telepathic communication. It's all through thoughts.

Has it ever happened that you were thinking of someone, and they called or texted you right then? You were in the same thought wavelength as the other person, both of you "picking up" thoughts from the other.

It's similar to how a radio works. If we tune to a country music station, we'll hear country music. If we tune into a talk radio station, we'll hear talk radio. Simple, right?

Every radio program is broadcast on a different frequency. The radio is actually a receiver of the frequency.

All frequencies exist at the same time. You'll hear what you tune into. The same concept applies when we want to have real conversations with our loved ones in Spirit.

We need to become better receivers.

As a medium, I'm not always open to receiving Spirit thoughts. My focus isn't always there.

When I'm at the grocery store, I'm not picking up on anybody's loved ones in Spirit. I'm thinking about the things on my grocery list.

Connecting with Spirit takes getting quiet, tuning in, receiving.

Spirit will come through for you. You've got to be patient with yourself. It's like learning a new language.

Are you willing to get quiet? Are you willing to receive?

CHAPTER 11

AM I MAKING IT UP?

Learning to trust is a spiritual muscle that you can strengthen.

One of the biggest obstacles is getting our li'l "monkey mind" out of the way.

You'll want to dismiss what you receive because you're sure "that's what they'd say to me anyway. I'm just making it up."

I started writing in a diary when I was five years old. I'd write about the math test we had at school, about the stitches that my classmate got on his tongue, about Uncle French bringing a baby elephant home to Buffy and Jodie on my favorite TV show *Family Affair*, and about how my mom made fried chicken and rice pilaf when our cousins came over for dinner that night.

It was about recording events.

In junior high and high school, my writing was about the latest crush I had, and all the insecurities I had. (And I had lots of them!) In my 20s, my writing mostly rambled on about what I was going through with different jobs, what I was feeling, what diet I was trying, and why I didn't feel like I fit in in this world. It was messy, emotional, sometimes happy, often whiny.

I didn't always feel better. I often felt like I was just swimming around in muck and putting it on paper.

A couple years before my first child, Ariana, was born, I started writing with my angels. I didn't know who they were, but I trusted that we all had a team of angels around us, and I was curious about how they might be able to support me.

All I asked was, "My dearest Angels of God, what would you like me to know today?"

The tone of what came through in the writing was so different. The messages were always loving, uplifting, gentle, and encouraging. Every single time I wrote with them. And I always felt better after writing.

I was learning to receive. I didn't question it because I knew it didn't sound like me at all!

This is how you'll know—by the tone, the energy of the words. Spirit won't ever use a negative or harsh tone with you . . . ever.

Let's try something.

Say your whole name to yourself . . . silently.

Did you hear that inside of your head? The thought of your name?

Now think of the song "Row, Row, Row Your Boat" and sing it to yourself . . . silently.

Can you hear that?

That's similar to how you'll "hear" Spirit's thoughts for you. It might seem like your own thoughts. The biggest difference is the loving tone that comes from Spirit. And the more we practice, the more you will let go and trust.

Are you ready?

Who in Spirit would you love to have a conversation with?

Write your thoughts here.

CHAPTER 12

YOU'RE READY . . . LET'S DO THIS!

*Take time for quiet moments. Spirit speaks
through whispered thought.*

Sometimes my clients have been hesitant to have conversations with Spirit because they just don't know what to ask. You can ask them anything. The key is to be open and willing to receive their answer.

Here are some questions you can start with.

Are you ok?

Do you hear me?

Are you proud of me?

Do you know how much I love you?

How can I connect with you more clearly?

How do you understand religion now?

How do you see death now? What's it like without a physical body?

How do you see life from your perspective now? Is there anything you'd do differently?

Is there a message you'd like me to deliver to someone else?

What would be most helpful for me to remember today?

Is there anything that's keeping me stuck in my life?

Can you help me see this fear of _____ differently?

How can I best serve others?

Feel free to use one of these, or any other question you'd love to ask!

You don't have to worry too much about the where or when.

I have conversations with Spirit in my home, in my car, in the shower, at a coffee shop, anywhere. Wherever you are, you can tune in to Spirit. For right now, we're going to focus on having a written conversation with a person in Spirit.

You've got the desire to tune in and a willingness to receive. It's time to get quiet. Go where you won't be distracted by anybody or any pets.

Silence your phone, get cozy, and get some paper and a pen. (Or you can print out the page I've provided for you.)

It's certainly not necessary, but if you'd like, you can have a picture of the person or light a candle.

Focus on your breath in and out. Take a few deep breaths.

Imagine being surrounded in a beautiful energy of light. (You can choose the color.)

Sense that light around you. You can relax right into that light. You want to be in a state of relaxed openness of your mind and of your heart.

Bring your awareness into your heart and breathe.

Affirm: *I surrender attachment to the outcome and trust that I'll receive what is in the highest and greatest good of all concerned. Spirit, I welcome you here with me. Thank you.*

What would you really, really like to ask?

Stay in your heart. Be open to the truth, and you'll receive it.

Breathe. Relax. Imagine your heart opening to receive.

Now put your pen to the paper.

> Dear (your loved one in Spirit), then write out your question.
>
> Example: *Dear Mom, are you ok?*

After you write your question, breathe, listen and allow. Your response may come as thoughts that pop into your awareness. You might get an image that drops in. You might have an inner knowing. You can simply allow your pen to move without trying to hear it first.

The key is to allow, allow, allow.

You'll start the response with:

> Dear (your own name), I love you and . . .
>
> Example: *Dear Sandy, I love you and yes, of course, I'm ok honey! I'm always with you. I'm right here with you . . .*

Write whatever comes to you. Don't censor it, don't judge it. Don't worry if it's going to make sense or not. If it's one sentence, one word, a paragraph, or a page, great.

Accept it even if you may feel like you're making it up. Sometimes I blur my eyes when I'm doing this writing so that I'm not attached to what I'm receiving.

Trust it. Honor your first impressions, impulses, and feelings.

Remember, this is a back-and-forth conversation you can have. Feel free to ask a question for clarification.

And then, offer gratitude for the experience.

Do this every day for a week and notice how it starts to flow more. Then do it as often as you'd like. Remember you're not bothering anyone.

Your turn . . .

Dear _____,

Dear _____, I love you and . . .

Notice the tone of the conversation. How does it feel to you? What is the feeling that comes through the words?

CHAPTER 13

NOW WHAT?

How would you love to live this precious life?

Spirit understands life from a different perspective. There's no judgment, no painful regret about how one has lived, because those in Spirit know they did the best they could, at the level of awareness they were in. There is no ego anymore, only pure love.

When they offer guidance, there are four common themes I hear over and over again. As you read them, pause and think about how you'd like to live your life going forward.

Here's what they've shared:

1. They can see that they spent so much time worried and afraid. And what is clear to them now is that there was really nothing to fear. Everything always had a way of working itself out. They want to remind us that every experience is meant for our growth and learning. When we know this, we can relax more.

2. They can see that they let small moments pass by unnoticed or unappreciated because life was so busy. Sunsets, smiles, small acts of kindness. Little miracles every day. They urge us to slow down and notice more. When we do, we'd have more moments of peace.

3. They can see how they played small or lived inauthentically because of fear. Fear of failure, fear of rejection, fear of disappointing others. They point us to live true to our hearts and live in a way that makes us happy.

4. They can see how God's presence was always with them, never separate from them. They now know that God's energy is much bigger than any fear. They want us to remember that, and that there is a still small voice within that is always guiding us. It is our inner GPS.

Death is not the end of them.

Grief is not the end of you.

You're never alone.

My hope and my prayer is that this book has touched you in some way, so that you see death and life differently

May you live life in a way that makes *you* proud, my friend.

This is the end of the book . . . or is it?

FROM MY JOURNAL:

Death,

You are a great teacher . . . a quick catalyst for truth.

You are a no-bullshit zone.

You come in and clear out.

You help us to see what really matters.

You are so feared because we were taught to fear you.

You represent the end.

But you also represent the beginning.

You represent total union with God . . . the awareness of the soul's perfection.

You are a beautiful de-conditioner . . . releasing one from their stories.

You are a welcome respite from emotional and physical pain.

You seem to be a separator, separating people from their loved ones.

And that is the fear.

Fear of separation.

> Death's response ...
>
> *To all, you have feared me, but in truth what you are afraid of is your story about me.*
>
> *You live in fear of separation.*
>
> *Separation from worthiness, love, money, time, God.*
>
> *That is what scares you.*
>
> *Loss ... touches that fear of separation.*
>
> *Truth is ... I am a great connector.*
>
> *Reconnection to God, to Source, to one's soul.*
>
> *Watch the "I will never ..." stories that pop up when I am present.*
>
> *None are true.*
>
> *I am here as a reminder of love. I am here to bring you Home to love ... to your True Self.*
>
> *There is nothing to fear.*

ABOUT THE AUTHOR

Sandy Alemian is a spiritual guide, who helps people understand life and death from a higher perspective, one with far less fear.

As a rare combination of Spirit Medium, Life Coach, and Hypnotist (specializing in past life regression), Sandy helps you get clear and aligned with a life that you'd love.

She is the author of two other books, *Congratulations . . . It's an Angel* and *WHAT was God Thinking?!*

She has 3 children: Ariana, Tia, and her baby angel Talia.

Sandy was born in Massachusetts, where she currently resides with her husband, until it gets cold in New England, and then they snowbird in Naples, Florida.

To contact Sandy, please reach out through her website: www.sandyalemian.com

For more information about the author, please visit:

Facebook: https://www.facebook.com/sandy.alemian
YouTube: https://www.youtube.com/sandyalemian
Instagram: @sandyalemian

Check out other books by Sandy Alemian on Amazon.com:

Congratulations... It's an Angel

WHAT was God Thinking?!

Made in the USA
Columbia, SC
19 December 2022

dc870fce-9a64-4a1e-8eff-949ad5305df1R01